MUSIC
MINUS
ONE

BOOKS BY JANE SHORE

The Minute Hand (*1987*)

Eye Level (*1977*)

Poems
by
Jane
Shore

MUSIC
MINUS
ONE

Picador USA
New York

MUSIC MINUS ONE. Copyright © 1996 by Jane Shore. All rights reserved. Printed in the United States of America. No part of this book may be used or reproduced in any manner whatsoever without written permission except in the case of brief quotations embodied in critical articles or reviews. For information, address Picador USA, 175 Fifth Avenue, New York, NY 10010.

Production Editor: David Stanford Burr

Designer: Pei Loi Koay

Picador® is a U.S. registered trademark and is used by St. Martin's Press under license from Pan Books Limited.

Library of Congress Cataloging-in-Publication Data

Shore, Jane.
    Music minus one : poems / by Jane Shore.—1st ed.
            p.   cm.
    ISBN 0-312-14686-8 (trade cloth)
    I. Title.
    PS3569.H5795M87   1996
    811'.54—dc20   96-17315
    Shore   /404898   CIP

First Picador USA Edition: September 1996

10   9   8   7   6   5   4   3   2   1

In memory of my parents

Essie Shore

(1915–1991)

and George Shore

(1915–1993)

ACKNOWLEDGMENTS

Grateful acknowledgment is made to the editors of the following magazines in which versions of these poems appeared or will appear: *The New Republic,* "Last Breath"; *Ploughshares,* "Monday," "Workout"; *Salmagundi,* "Peak Season"; *The Virginia Quarterly Review,* "Washing the Streets of Holland," "Music Minus One"; *The G. W. Review,* "Missing."

An earlier version of "The Bad Mother" first appeared in *Her Face in the Mirror, Jewish Women on Mother and Daughters,* edited by Faye Moskowitz, Beacon Press, 1994.

A few lines in "A Vision" are loosely quoted from E. H. Gombrich's *The Story of Art,* Phaidon Press, 1962.

I would like to thank The John Simon Guggenheim Foundation, The Alfred Hodder Foundation, The National Endowment for the Arts, and The George Washington University for their support during the completion of this collection.

Special thanks to Lorrie Goldensohn, to Jody Bolz, Louise Glück, Ellen Voigt, Carol Muske, Stuart Dybek, and to my husband, Howard Norman.

CONTENTS

3

4

"The writer needs an address,

very badly needs an address—

that is his roots.

—Isaac Bashevis Singer

MUSIC *MINUS* ONE

When I was twelve, I read *The Diary of Anne Frank.*
I identified with her having to live
stories above a busy street
over a business, and having to keep quiet
for hours at a time.
I'd pad about on tiptoe,
trying not to disturb the customers
shopping in my parents' dress store below,
their voices drifting up through the floorboards.
I'd pretend I was eavesdropping
from Anne's attic, while downstairs,
life went on without me.

That winter a frozen pipe cracked,
thawed, then flooded the cellar under the store.
Broken mannequins lay in heaps
and rats scuttled up through the drain.
My old books, old dolls, stuffed animals
bobbed among the giant torsos.

When the water receded,
I dredged up a china plate,
sole survivor of the Blue Willow tea set
I had when I was six.
Its boat and bridge and willow plumes,
its turtledoves hovering above a pagoda roof,
were glazed the same delft-blue as the windmills
on our tile hot plate made in Holland.

My family admired the Dutch people;
they'd hidden Jews in their houses during the War.
Once, while I was playing with my tea set,
I heard my aunt Roz say that exact thing:
"The Dutch hid Jews during the War."
My aunts and uncles sat in the living room,
arguing the Holocaust—the inevitable subject—
who had helped and who had not.
A moment later, our German cleaning lady,
Mrs. Herman—my mother liked her—
literally scrubbed her way past,
on hands and knees, dragging her pail and rags.
My aunt Lil spoke a few sentences in Yiddish.
"What did you say?" I begged her.
Mrs. Herman had just rolled up the oval rug.
My aunt said, "Germans were bad. The Dutch were good."

"And the streets of Holland are immaculate,"
my mother said, "because every morning
the Dutch wash their sidewalks down."

And so I made up a game I called
"Washing the Streets of Holland."
During my bath I'd climb out of the tub,
and sprinkle Old Dutch Cleanser on the floor.
I'd hold my breath, careful
not to inhale the deadly powder.
The Dutch Cleanser lady wore a bonnet
whose flaps completely hid her face.
In her clogs and blue skirts and clean white apron,
and with a raised stick, about to strike,
she was chasing something—or someone—
on the other side of the can.

Chases Dirt, the label said.

Naked on my hands and knees,
I'd scrub the floor with a washcloth
until my bathwater turned cold.
There was a lot of dirt in Holland;
but I was doing my part to help.
One night, my father yelled from behind the door,
"What are you doing in there?"
I was washing the streets of Holland.

Blue woman on the powder can,
blue willowware plate,
gentle brushstrokes of the pagoda roof,
blades of windmills, glazed waters of the lagoon,
blue tattoo inked in flesh,
blue ink in a diary,
blue ocean whose water is really colorless, like tears,
a flood of tears, all seven seas running together—
blurring the words
and washing them away.

My father sways before the mirror
in the blue tiled bathroom, shaving.
The wide legs of his boxer shorts
empty as wind socks,
the neck of his white cotton undershirt
fringed with curly black hairs.

Overnight his shaving brush
has stiffened into the shape of a flame.
When he swirls it around in the mug,
the bristles plump up with lather,
as if he's folding egg whites into batter.

The empty razor lies open-jawed
in a puddle of milky water.
The double-edged blades come packed
in envelopes of five, each blade
wrapped separately in thin waxed paper
like a stick of gum.

My father glances at the mirror
like a woman applying makeup;
then paints on a mustache and beard
leaving only a thin mouth hole.
His lips look redder against the foam.
.He lathers his chin, his Adam's apple,
the pebbly skin of his throat.

Scraping, he works quickly, in silence,
in distracted concentration,
the same way he eats his dinner every night.
But what is making my mild father so angry,
arguing with the man on the glass?
He stretches his lips into the widest
possible smile, then bares
his teeth in a grimace.

He nicks himself. Here and there,
the lather is flecked with threads of blood.
Then stroke by stroke, my father's face
gradually returns to him,
so raw and tender I ache to touch.
What in the world would harm him now,
looking as he does, with shreds
of toilet tissue stuck on his face like feathers,
each one glued with a small red dot.

"Jane lived in a big white house
with a garden and a yard
and an apple tree out back."
Waiting my turn to read

out loud before the class,
my wooden desk and chair
bolted to the wooden floor,
Jane skipped and jumped and ran.

Jane—my very name—
was all we had in common.
Jane's mother knitted socks.
Mine couldn't knit a stitch.

Jane and Dick—her brother—
a matched pair
of salt and pepper shakers,
ate dinner

opposite each other;
Father facing Mother.
Two parents, two children, two pets.
My sister wasn't born yet.

Big *A* and little *a,*
upper- and lowercase *B,*
the sibling alphabet
paraded across the chalkboard

white on black, a negative
of my primer's printed page—
the page I'd read at home,
the passage I knew by heart—

where the kitten, Puff,
jumps into the sewing basket,
bats her paw and chases
a rolling ball of yarn

across the kitchen floor
and gets all tangled up.
Who'd be the lucky one
to read it to the class?

A dozen hands shot up
except Lucille's, and mine.
Shiny straight black hair,
patent leather Mary Janes,

black cat's-eye frames
studded with rhinestones—
Lucille was special.
She couldn't read or spell.

She'd had to repeat
the first grade twice,
but received straight *A*'s
for perfect attendance.

Glazed, she stared
at the erased blackboard,
a swirling Milky Way.
The teacher skipped Lucille

and called out, "Jane!"
I snapped back to my book,
the kitten, sewing basket,
and ball of yarn.

I opened my mouth to read
the page fate gave to me.
Not wanting to show off,
I stumbled—on purpose—

on the words *I knew* I knew,
and got all tangled up
in that rolling ball of yarn
unraveling its line

of looping handwriting
across the kitchen floor
Mother scrubbed and waxed
upon her hands and knees.

—Jane's mother, not mine.
Mine puffed on her cigarette,
smoke scribbling on the air
in the rooms we call our lives

where it begins to snow
real snow outside the panes,
beyond the huge paper flakes
children fold, cut and tape

onto classroom windows,
no two flakes alike:
brief fingerprints
whorling on the glass.

I was miserable every day that summer
at Camp Bell, summer of the iron lung
and Joe McCarthy. Miserable
eating my kosher lunch and playing tag
in scratchy new shorts, my name repeated
on the labels my mother whipstitched
to the stiff elastic waistbands of my underpants.
The pool gleamed, dangerous and inviting . . .
I could catch polio from the locker room's
wet concrete floor, the pint-sized toilets
behind rustic swinging doors.

I'd be so much happier staying at home
playing with my Tiny Tears Doll,
and watching Catholic boys who smoked and swore
playing stickball in the alley behind our store,
their hair slicked back in long DAs.
Camp Bell's yeshiva boys
wore velvet and satin skullcaps
the size of the saucers in my china tea set;
some were crocheted like doilies
and held in place with a bobby pin.

There were days I'd be so homesick, I'd dawdle
behind my group, the Peewees,
whimpering on the path of our nature walks,
the Manhattan skyline hovering in the east
in its dirty snarl of cloud.
Bending over a stream, combing the shallows

for tadpoles, in the swirling mirror of water
I'd suddenly see my mother—
her scuffs, her terry cloth robe—
anything could set me off.

It was easy to spot other crybabies,
bloodshot eyes and splotchy skin,
hiccuping and sobbing out in the open.
A few sat on the toilet and bawled
in the privacy of a bathroom stall.
One ingenious boy made a "church"—
by folding his hands together, as if in prayer,
over his nose and mouth
into which he'd slide his thumb, and suck.
His straightened pinkies raised the steeple.

He'd walk from Baseball to Arts-and-Crafts,
from Rowing to Swimming to Volleyball,
all day clamping his hands
like an oxygen mask over his face.
The steeple jutted up between his eyes
as each day he erected his sanctuary,
breathing the air of his own consoling breath.

My first best friend had pale delicate skin
and when she laughed or was embarrassed
her cheeks flared up into two hot pink spots
for hours, like stains she couldn't rub out.
Her house was walking-distance from the firehouse,
so the days and nights her father was on duty,
she could visit him anytime she wanted
in the private quarters on the second floor
above the gleaming trucks and coiled hoses
where her father lived his other life.
When I first went along with Cynthia,
I thought I'd have to shinny up the brass pole
through the hole cut in the ceiling,
but we only had to walk up stairs, to see
one big happy family of men, smoking,
playing cards around the dining table,
cooking sausages on the stove for dinner,
among the lined-up pairs of boots
and socks drying on radiators, and heavy
black rubber coats hanging on hooks,
flayed open, smooth as animal hides.
In the dormitory, I saw their beds made
with linens from home, the shelf of personal
belongings, children's photos, lucky stones.
They let me pet their mascot Dalmatian while
Cynthia kissed each one of them good-bye.
Afternoons after school, we'd play quietly
in the rose garden behind her house,
so as not to wake her father, off-duty.
Once, stumbling outside in his pajamas,

he looked perfectly ordinary, thin and pale,
just like my own father who worked regular
hours—but with red-rimmed watery
blue eyes as if he'd just been crying,
his five o'clock shadow colorless as ice.
Blushing, Cynthia caught me staring at him,
and cut in, "He's not really a lazy bones—
he's just catching up on his sleep."
When a small plane crashed one foggy morning
into the WOR Radio Tower twelve blocks away,
and the engine sailed over town
and landed down the street from us,
burning an apartment house to the ground,
many people died, all the passengers.
From my bedroom window I could see smoke,
and, in the distance, eleven stories high,
the tower's torn and twisted scaffolding
where the plane had caught in it like a fly.
A week later, walking with Cynthia after school,
she whispered that her father, the day after
the crash, sifting through the cooling rubble
in the vacant lot next door, saw something
lying in the dirt, he didn't know what,
and picked up a woman's hand severed
at the wrist, a left hand, with a diamond
engagement ring still on it. For months
the remaining fuselage lodged in the tower
like a decomposing corpse, until someone
figured out a way to bring it down.

My chicken pox was itchy, like pinfeathers.
Blisters popped out on my scalp, eyelids, even my tongue,
like the plague God brought down on Egypt.
"Don't scratch!" my mother yelled.
I couldn't help but scratch.

Quarantined from my new baby sister,
I was playing in the sunroom Easter Sunday morning,
keeping track of the parade on the television,
I was playing in the sunroom the whole week before,
during Passover, while I was still contagious,
I was playing in the sunroom a month before,
the one and only time I met my grandfather—
a cameo appearance—him all tanned and leathery
like a retired movie star,
bringing a crate of Florida grapefruit for the family
and a stuffed baby chick for me.

The moment I saw the chick—
its fake black eyes,
its real beak smooth as a shelled peanut
with two little slits for nostrils—
I was afraid of it.
Its insides had been scooped out
like the chickens my mother koshered,
sticking her hand between the legs and pulling out
the shiny gizzard, liver and the gigantic ruby
of the heart, then rubbing the skin and inside cavity
with Diamond Crystal Kosher Salt.

What scared me most
was that the chick was really dead
in its *actual* body, like a mummy;
its precious organs thrown away,
its body sanitized, stuffed with straw,
and covered with feathers dyed a sunny yellow.

I was sure I'd caught the chicken pox
from the baby chick.
I thought I'd die.

On the first Passover,
the Angel of Death had slaughtered
every Egyptian firstborn.
Smeared blood was the sign
for the Angel to pass over.

I was the firstborn.
My body was covered with signs.

Outside the sunroom windows,
they were walking home from church
to eat their holiday dinners:
men and boys in somber suits,
women in flowered hats,
girls wearing new spring coats I'd seen on racks
at Lobels Department Store,
in those lovely Easter egg colors—the unbleached wool
dipped into pale washes
of baby blue, mint, lavender, and pink—

pink as an Easter ham
stuck all over with cloves,

cloves like the burning scabs I scratched
as they paraded past.

I wheeled my baby sister to the park.
The baseball diamond deserted,
a dusty wavering mirage.
It was hot, so hot
the Chamber of Commerce
canceled the annual chicken barbecue,
the coals already burning
under the empty grills.

My father closed up early.
We lounged around all afternoon
in our apartment over the store.
My mother wore her sheerest bra and panties.
My father stripped to his boxer shorts.
He sat at the kitchen table in the path of the fan;
like a game of solitaire, the ticket stubs—
the week's receipts—before him.

I was cutting out a family of paper dolls,
wool winter coats and hats,
the daughter's organdy party dress.
My elbows stuck to the vinyl tablecloth,
my thighs to the vinyl cushions.
I was wearing the thick cotton underpants
I'd worn throughout my childhood,
my chest bare in front of my father
for the very last time.

The Cold War was on TV.
My scissors cut along the shoulders, hips,
the perfect neutral bodies.
The Father didn't have my father's bald spot,
nor the Mother my mother's belly.
Their modest children—a girl and a boy—
had underwear painted onto their skin.

I cut out their split-level house in the country,
their collie, their crew-cut lawn.
I cut out their flagstone patio, shady backyard.
The kit even had a fallout shelter
with walls of painted shelves
filled with canned goods and bottled water.

Too hot to talk, too hot to eat,
we lowered the blinds
and sat in the dark all day and evening—
turning on lamps only made more heat.
We camped out on the living room sofa.
Ozzie and Harriet. Canned laughter. The News.
The station signed off, jets flew in formation
to the strains of the national anthem.

When the peacock's tail feathers fanned out,
an array of grays,
my father flicked the dial.
We watched a white dot fade and shrink to nothing
in the center of the blackened screen.
Finally, we all tried to sleep.
My mother lay down in the twin bed

across from mine, on top of her separate sheet,
dabbing her forehead with a cold washcloth.

During the night the fever broke.
Only juice for breakfast.
At ten A.M., in shorts and a halter,
I went downstairs with my father.
He unlocked the store—
thirty seconds to turn off the alarm.
Inside smelled stuffy, like a closet.
He got the big ceiling fan going; cooling air
rustled through the dress racks.

I had left my mother working at the kitchen table
pasting up the ad for Sunday's paper,
snipping and gluing the cutout models on the page,
under CORDUROY VILLAGE SUMMER SALE 20% OFF.

While my father dusted the counter,
I modeled jewelry for no one.
The first customer walked in about eleven.
Formal to the end, under his suit jacket,
my father wore a short-sleeved shirt
and kept his tie tied until closing.

One year, when business was bad,
our next door neighbor, Jack,
set fire to his bakery.
He started it small, in the cellar, with oily rags,
and when he saw them smolder
he must have run upstairs past his darkened store's
empty ovens, empty cash register,
up to his apartment on the second floor
and phoned the firehouse four blocks away.

He did it in the middle of the night.
My mother shook me awake
gently, so I wouldn't panic,
whispering, "Grab the bird cage!"
No time to pack my jewelry box
or change out of my pajamas,
I heard banging on our downstairs door,
shouts and smashing glass,
the building shaking as the firemen chopped holes
in the flat tarred bakery roof.

The cops herded my family out into the street,
brilliantly lit, a corner of the night torn open,
ladders telescoping into the sky.
My father carried the sleeping baby.
My mother clutched her pocketbook against her coat,
her nightgown showing below the hem.
As we rushed past the windows of our store,
mannequins in evening dress
stared blankly at our sudden exodus.

In the Tavern Bar and Grill,
the only place open that late at night,
I sat in a booth and sipped my Coke
with Jack's two boys, and the butcher's,
the grocer's, and the druggist's kids,
who lived in their apartments over their stores,
while the regulars smoked at the bar,
joking with the bartender:
salesmen, drunks, divorcées,
characters I'd watched on late-night movies.

They put it out before it spread too far.
We closed the store for inventory, and the next day,
had a fire sale of the smoke-damaged stock.
My father swept glass from the sidewalk,
piled a card table with sweaters and scarves,
then rolled out racks of dresses
in front of our shop.

Upstairs, even with the windows open,
the smoke made our eyes water, chafed throats raw,
every breath insisting we remember.
Weeks later, as I dressed for school,
I'd open a bureau drawer and unfold
a ghost of smoke from my underwear.
And at night, bathroom door closed
and the shower on hot,
standing before the mirror filling up with steam,
I could swear my body was robed in smoke
growing darker and darker every year.

The electric eye of the mezuzah
guarded our apartment over the store
as innocent of Christmas
as heaven, where God lived,
how many stories above the world?
Was He angry when He saw
all the windows on my street—
the assimilated grocer's, druggist's,
even my father's store—lit up
like windows in an Advent calendar?

Alone in my bedroom
the nights my parents worked late,
I'd hear voices and laughter
floating up through the floor—
customers trying on dressy dresses
in the fitting rooms below.
The store was dressed up, too,
with tinsel, icicles,
everything but a Christmas tree—
"Over my dead body," my mother said.

Christmas was strictly business
in my parents' store.
Fourteen shopping days to go,
my class sang carols
in front of the school assembly.
In starched white blouses
we marched up to the stage,
our mouths a chain of O's.
When we came to the refrain,
"Christ the Savior is born,"

as if on cue all the Jewish kids
were silent, except me,
absentmindedly humming along
until the word *Christ* slipped out.
It was an accident!
Gentiles believed in Christ.
We Jews believed in a God
Whose face we were forbidden to see,
Whose name we were forbidden
to say out loud, or write completely.

We had to spell it *G-d,*
the missing *o* dashing into its hole.
That afternoon after school,
I sat near an empty fitting room
folding cardboard gift boxes,
carefully locking the flaps in place.
Was God going to punish me?
My father knelt in the window display
among the mannequins,
like one of the Magi in a crèche,

dusting a plastic angel three feet tall.
Stored in the cellar under the stairs,
draped in her dusty cellophane caul,
waiting to be reborn,
she lorded it over the old mannequins,
naked, bald, their amputated limbs
piled in the corner like firewood.
The Sunday before the holiday season
she ascended, one floor, to the store,
trailing a tail of electric cord.

After my father plugged her in,
she glowed from halo-tip to toe,
faith—a fever—warming her cheeks,
her insides lit by a tiny bulb.
I longed to smuggle her up to my room,
to have some company at night
when the store was open late.
I gazed down the darkening street,
Seventy-ninth to Boulevard East,
and out over the Hudson.

At sundown, I went upstairs.
Dinner was defrosting in the oven.
The last night of Chanukah,
eight candles, like eight crayons,
wobbled in the brass menorah.
My father struck the match.
Flame wavering in my hand,
I lit the candles from right
to left, like a line of Hebrew writing,
and numbly sang the blessing

as if the words on my breath
could sweep away the word
I'd sung earlier that day.
Was God going to punish me?
I'd have to ask the Magic 8 Ball,
my gift the first night of Chanukah.
For the last seven nights,
before going to sleep,
instead of saying my prayers,
I'd consulted the 8 Ball.

It could predict the future.
You asked it a yes-or-no question,
you turned it over,
and the answer slowly floated up
through the inky liquid
to the round window on top.
I held the black ball
firmly in my hands.
"Is God going to punish me?"
"CONCENTRATE AND ASK AGAIN"

I stared out my bedroom window
across the back alley
at the rabbi's house,
and watched him walk from room
to room, his windows
like frames on a strip of film.
He vanished through his kitchen door
and reappeared a moment later
a shadow, a hazy nimbus rippling
his bathroom's glazed window glass.

Swaying before his mirrored ark's
two fluorescent scrolls of light,
he performed his evening ritual—
brushing his teeth,
washing his hands, then
sinking discreetly out of sight.
For spying on the rabbi,
I'd added on another sin!
I concentrated, closed my eyes,
again, I asked the question:

"Is God going to punish me?"
"REPLY HAZY   TRY AGAIN"
"Is God going to punish me?"
"BETTER NOT TELL YOU NOW"
"Is God going to punish me?"
"IT IS DECIDEDLY SO"
"Is God going to punish me?"
"MY REPLY IS NO"
"8 Ball, what is your answer?"
"ASK AGAIN LATER"

I had to see what was inside.
I took a hammer to the ball,
and whacked. Not a crack;
I'd barely scratched its shell.
I looked into its eye,
the dark unblinking eye,
as far as I could see inside the skull
where, floating together in ink
(so many I couldn't see them all)
were all the answers possible.

2

Jetting safely from the Jews in New Jersey
to the Jews in Miami Beach,
my mother and aunt and I
took a week's vacation at the Hotel Seville.
We'd left the men back home.

Every morning after breakfast,
we'd head for the pool, weaving
through rows of recumbent sunbathers,
the lounge chairs filling up as fast
as cemetery plots in Queens.

My mother and aunt unfurled their towels.
They ordered iced drinks from the bar.
They took turns greasing each other's backs
with tanning lotion white as semen,
gently, gently, rubbing it in.

I snapped my rubber bathing cap
under my chin, tucking in my ponytail,
and inched down the ladder into the pool
aquamarine as the birthstone ring
I'd left in our hotel room, for safekeeping.

Icy water lapped the shivering yardstick
of my body, climbing my thighs, my belly,
the two flat buttons on my chest.
Wading toward the deep end,
my feet brushed the tile floor, sloping

like the Embassy Theater's back home,
on whose giant screen Esther Williams,
the Jewish movie star and beauty queen,
dived off a cliff into a CinemaScope lagoon
steeped in gallons of blue food coloring:

palm trees, sunsets, a paradise like here.
Like her, I smiled, stroking the water,
while a boy cannonballed off the board,
a boy I'd seen eating breakfast
in the hotel restaurant with his family—

as well behaved as a bar mitzvah boy.
Braces gleaming beneath his faint mustache,
he teased me with splashes, showing off
the way the boys at school punched girls
they liked. He did handstands in the water.

Popping up, he pushed my head under,
hard, like a plunger; no time for a breath
as the furious, headless body held me down.
The day before, when we toured
Parrot Jungle, I saw a short brown man

step into a sand pit, unstrap his belt,
and bind an alligator's enormous jaws.
Flipping her over, he rubbed her belly,
while in a neighboring cage, on stage,
a parrot pirouetted on a swing, and cockatoos

and macaws preened and chattered on.
Thrashing under, my mouth clamped shut
against the churned-up luminescent blue,
my legs, pale blue-veined marble,
pale as the hand that held me down

long enough to show me who was boss.
Long enough for my head to shatter the glass roof
of water, and we could be ourselves again—
a boy and a girl—not mortal enemies—
years before we'd enter the world for real.

Sometimes when I pick up a razor and shave my legs,
I remember that summer in Rockland Lake, New York,
and my mother's admonition:
"If you start shaving your legs now,
for the rest of your life the hair will grow back
thick and black and ugly, like a man's!"
Lucky for me, she never found my father's razor blade
I'd sandwiched between my mattress and box spring.
That was the summer I slept on the studio couch
in my little sister's room
at Applebaum's Bungalow Colony—
twenty white bungalows divided in half,
a pool, a tennis court, and a casino.
When my mother was out shopping or tanning by the pool
or playing mah-jongg with the other lonely wives,
I'd lock the bathroom door
and shave my legs one hair at a time,
the naked blade peppering my shins with cuts
I told her were mosquito bites.
That was the summer I got my first bra
and studied "142 Ways To Be Popular,"
a pamphlet distributed with acne soap.
At night under my steamy tent of blankets,
I read *Strangers When We Meet,*
enthralled by the scenes in motels, the guilty
adulterers kissing each other, and worse.
That was the summer my nightmare began:
a stranger in a tan fedora
stood outside the screen and stared at me;

menacing, but only staring.
A stocking mask of white latex stretched
over his eyes, his nose, his mouth.

On Friday evenings, the fathers would return to us
dead tired, from working all week in the city.
Soldiers on furlough from no war,
they'd drive up to the country,
only forty-five minutes away.
Changed into Bermuda shorts and aprons,
they'd carry platters of scored meat
to the brick barbecue pits out back.
Then dusk and smoke and the smell of burning
sifted through the screens,
the tinfoil jackets of the Idahos,
precious glintings among the coals.

The Shangri La Bungalow Colony up the road
imported professionals from the Catskills
to star in their weekend shows—
singers, magic acts, and stand-up comics
like Morey Amsterdam and Henny Youngman.
But at Applebaum's Bungalow Colony,
every Friday night, we played bingo,
every Saturday night, we put on a talent show.

In the end-of-the-season gala,
our next-door neighbor, Mrs. Greenberg,
a retired chorus girl "still in great shape
for fifty-six years old,"
tap-danced to Mr. Bloom's trombone solo;
followed by The Amazing Zimmerman—

a medical student from Brooklyn
—Sol Zimmerman's son, from Bungalow 24—
who, just by holding his hand to his forehead
and concentrating,
could bend spoon, such a genius.
And last of all, my mother's skit
inspired by the Broadway musical, *South Pacific,*
where my father had fought in the War.
(That morning, my mother had drafted the men
from pinochle and golf
and drilled them in secret all day,
shooing us kids away from the knotty-pine casino.)

When Mrs. Applebaum sat down at the piano
and played the opening bars
of "Bloody Mary is the Girl I Love,"
a dozen husbands stormed the stage,
wearing grass skirts, and bras—two coconut shells
clamped over their hairy breasts.
Hairy potbellies, pale hairy legs,
their own skin was a kind of hirsute costume they wore
with their street shoes and black socks,
lipstick, wigs, and gag glasses
with eyeballs popping out and jiggling on springs.
It brought the house down.

That was the summer I had a job, baby-sitting
for a couple who'd had a baby late, at forty-two.
Playing catch one muggy Sunday before dinner,
my ball rolled under their bedroom window,
curtains parting just enough for me to peek in and see
the baby sleeping in her crib, and on the big bed

the mother and father dressed in bathing suits, napping.
Only the sounds of breathing, and the window shade
slapping against the screen,
the little crocheted ring on a string
dancing and dancing in the breeze.

In junior high, I used to practice dying
in Ava Grodner's bedroom after school.
We'd hyperventilate twenty times, then bend over
holding our breath until we fainted.
I'd only be out for a second, or two,
then come to, back in northern New Jersey,
staring at Ava's fringed chenille bedspread,
her black and white saddle shoes under the bed.
Once, I actually knocked myself out
after I fainted, hitting my head on the floor.
I woke up, unlike Larry Cohen's mother
impaled by a flying beach umbrella in Asbury Park
the windy summer before his bar mitzvah.
"The will of God," the rabbi said.
One Saturday morning, after Larry and his father
davenned Kaddish with the elders
in Temple, the Cohens' curly red hair,
sore thumbs, in that sea of bobbing gray,
I caught the bus to Manhattan
for my lesson at the Metropolitan Opera House
School of Ballet. I sat behind the driver,
leaned my head against the humming glass
flashing with the street that I grew up on—
Noveck's Drugs, Wolf's Deli, Embassy Theater,
kids already lining up for the Saturday matinee.
In my high upholstered seat, I felt superior,
immune, as the bus lumbered through Guttenberg,
West New York, Union City, and Weehawken,
perched on the Palisades.
The Manhattan skyline glittered across the Hudson.

Traffic funneled into the three mouths
of the Lincoln Tunnel; buses filed into the fumes.
I gulped down my last breath of good air, and panicked.
The tunnel might spring a leak, the Russians
might bomb us and I'd be stuck down here
forever, my past behind me, my future
an eye of light dilating on the other side.
Passengers dozed over their *New York Posts*.
It would be just my luck to be dead,
while on the deck of a Circle Line Boat
cruising the choppy Hudson, tourists
were dancing the cha-cha right over my head.

I loved to shop at the Five-and-Ten,
the Woolworth's on Bergenline,
a block away from my parents' store.
Aiming at the aisle of School Supplies,
I'd browse up and down the narrow rows,
the acres of dusty merchandise
I'd memorized like multiplication tables.
Under the buzzing fluorescent lights,
I'd dawdle, until closing time.

Few items cost a nickel or a dime
on the aisle of Bargain Underwear,
one side women's, the other men's;
not nylon panties or boxer shorts,
not curlers or permanent waves,
depilatories or mustache bleach.
How old was I?—twelve . . . ? thirteen . . . ?
I wore a "bra"—a modified
cotton undershirt with straps—

purchased on the children's floor
at Lobels, where I'd bought
my Girl Scout uniform.
Not the kind I begged my mother for.
And not, in Comics and Magazines,
on the back page of *True Confessions*,
what Frederick's of Hollywood advertised:
bras with nipples playing peekaboo
and crotches slit for God-knows-what,

and for flat-chested girls,
the snow-peaked Himalayas of padded bras,
or the crème de la crème—
the Mark Eden Bust Developer—
mailed in a plain brown wrapper.
An old-maid manager patrolled the store
for shoplifters, perverts, and minors
haunting the glass case of falsies
displayed in matching pairs—

shaped like rubber toilet plungers,
they swelled from double A to double E.
The only girl I knew with breasts that big
was Nancy, my playmate until junior high,
who'd menstruated at the age of nine,
and at thirteen, in the seventh grade,
had given a miraculous virgin birth
to the "baby brother" her mother raised.
Girls who worked at the Five-and-Ten

also shopped at the Five-and-Ten
at one-third off. The girl dusting Aisle 4
wore a sweater sold on Aisle 8.
At five to six, they'd flash the lights
on and off like lightning.
I'd hurry past the salesgirl sweeping
feathers and seeds from Aisle 9,
where lovebirds and sickly parakeets
huddled in the dark after closing time.

I'd grab a No. 2 pencil, get in line,
and hand the cashier my only dime.
Her key ring dangling in the lock,
the manager inspected pocketbooks.
Then one by one, girls flew the coop,
and vanished in the souped-up cars
of boyfriends idling at the curb.
I had an inkling of what they did
in plush backseats on River Road.

I'd pass the "out-of-order" kiddie ride:
Thunder the Horse, who gobbled dimes,
and galloping, would hump like mad,
then quiver to a stop, mid-stride,
his hind legs lifting off the ground,
a crazy look in his marble eyes.
Thunder was always breaking down
long before your time was up,
a minute, while he rocked 'n' rolled.

A kick to his side would wake him up,
he'd shake for twenty seconds more,
neighing from a box inside,
then break down for a final time.
Once, instead of stopping still,
his heart went into overdrive
and he bucked like a wild stallion,
almost galloping off his pedestal,
while I held on, screaming, petrified,

until they pulled me off him,
yanked his plug, and he shuddered
abruptly, and died. I loved
his metal stirrups and his leather reins,
his carved saddle and carved flowing mane,
his bridle and real horsehair tail,
his flared nostrils and cracked hind hoof,
and, jammed into his panting mouth, the bit
rattling between his tongue and teeth.

In 1959, at Horace Mann Elementary
in North Bergen, New Jersey,
wearing white on Wednesday meant you were a virgin,
wearing red on Thursday meant you were a lesbian,
wearing green on Friday meant you were a tramp.

The gymnasium, with its locker room and showers
and drains, moldered in the basement.
Sanitary napkin dispensers were always empty,
and the changing room with stalls for privacy
had white flapping curtains that didn't quite close.
I undressed, and put on my gray cotton gymsuit
out in the open with all the other girls.

The gym teacher, Miss Piano, wore a Dutch-boy haircut.
Her legs were as solid as a baby grand's.
She called us by our last names, like privates in the army,
and clapped, as each girl climbed the ropes
and disappeared into girders and beams
and caged light fixtures on the ceiling.
When my turn came,
I gripped the lowest knot and dangled down;
my legs drawn up, I looked like a dying spider.

On wooden bleachers, chummy as sorority sisters
the lucky girls who had their periods
gossiped and did their homework
after handing Miss Piano a note from the nurse.
Where was my excuse?

After gym class, I'd undress in my own stall,
stuffing my gym suit back into its mildewed bag.
But first, I'd examine my underpants
for the red smear of "the curse."
The last of my friends, the last of the last.
No luck. I'd swathe myself again
in my neutral clothing.

When one morning, I woke up,
two black ink blots staining my pajamas,
I dragged my mother out of bed to tell her.
We squeezed into the bathroom
as if into our clubhouse,
as if she were about to show me the secret handshake.

Blushing, leaking, I sat on the tub's rim,
as if poised over the mikveh, the ritual bath.
Stuffed inside my underpants,
the bulky Kotex, safety pins, and elastic sanitary belt
I had stored in my closet for over a year.
My mother took a seat on the toilet lid.
"Ma," I shyly said, "I got my period,"
then leaned over to receive her kiss,
her blessing.

She looked as though she were going to cry.
In her blue nylon nightgown, her hairnet
a cobweb stretched over her bristling curlers,
my mother laughed, tears in her eyes,
and yelled, "Mazel Tov! Now you are a woman!
Welcome to the club!"

and slapped me across the face—
for the first and last time ever—

"*This* should be the worst pain you ever know."

The chartered bus took the ugly route
past the airport and the Jersey pike,
past cliffs some lovesick maniac climbed
to paint his girlfriend's initials
in dripping white.
I wanted to earn that badge so much—
the badge for Community Service—
I could see myself sewing it on
the sash of my Girl Scout uniform,
this wilting field of salad-green
my mother bought a size too large,
big enough to grow into.
I could see myself threading a needle,
and stitching the embroidered coin of cloth
in a circle of sutures until it held.

We braked outside the hospital gates.
My troop, a leader, and two chaperones
marched into the visitor's lounge,
single file through wire-mesh doors,
past folding chairs pushed against walls,
past punch bowls, stacked Dixie cups,
paper plates of Oreos and Social Teas
you'd see at any ordinary mixer.
A slow dance spun on the phonograph.
A fox-trot, then the stroll—
nothing wild, or excitable.

Where were the boys?
Only girls my age, and grown women,
a few pinheads and mongoloids
released in tandem like windup toys.
The girl I got was taller than me.
She placed her arm around my waist.
My left hand grazed her shoulder.
I knew it was impolite to stare
at her crooked teeth, her fraying collar,
white bobby sox, brown penny loafers,
plaid skirt and flowered blouse.
I'd never ever touched someone
who wore clothing that didn't match.

I wanted to ask her where she slept.
In a dormitory, in one big room
with other girls, a nightly slumber party?
Or locked up in solitary?
But I was too tongue-tied to ask.
And she never even looked at me
or smiled, or asked my name.
Counting out the fox-trot's beat,
she fitted her feet into invisible
rehearsed footprints on the floor.

I'd danced with other girls before
at weddings and bar mitzvahs,
cousins and aunts doing the hora,
the lindy, the mambo, the rhumba,
accompanied by a live orchestra;
and I'd danced with my girlfriends

in locked bedrooms—the radio on—
practicing leading my partner,
making her dip, making her whirl.

The sun had set, the room got dark.
Black stacks of wobbly 45s
lurched down the changer spindle.
We slow-danced for an hour or so
in a narrowing circle,
the girls in my Girl Scout troop
orbiting like a dozen moons.
Where oh where were our chaperones?

Couldn't they see how odd I felt?—
a cardboard cutout of a girl—
a girl who wore a uniform
every Monday night to meetings
in the basement of the Catholic Church
where we spread blankets on the cold
concrete floor, told ghost stories,
sang around the imaginary campfire—
things that normal girls would do—

as if normalcy were a badge you earned,
like a merit badge for cooking,
like the badge I'd surely earn tonight
for being a good citizen.
What on earth did my mother say—
dancing at the Officers Club
during the War when she joined the WACs—
to strangers on twenty-four-hour leave,
boys with faces shell-shocked as these?

Back on the bus, I chose a window seat,
and watched the dark landscape sliding by,
miles of refineries, smokestacks belching
clouds into the engorged backlit sky,
when out of the corner of my eye
I caught the eye of a ghostly girl
glazing the window's skin of glass—
that gaze of hers—familiar, strange.
Now I was one, and now the other,
caught in the somewhere in-between.

THE HOUSE OF SILVER BLONDES

Side by side in matching plastic capes,
my mother and I were two from a set
of Russian dolls wearing the family brand
of hair—dark, wavy brown.

A graduate of beauty school
was frosting my mother's hair today.
Only a few years older than I,
Angie had a honey-blonde beehive,
teased and glazed,
and a married boyfriend twice her age.

She stuffed my mother's hair
under a punctured bathing cap.
Her crochet hook pulled the dark strands
one by one through the holes.
At first my mother looked bald.
And then like one of those dolls
with rooted hair you can really comb,
clumps of hair plugged into the holes
drilled in rows around their skulls.

Pulling on her rubber gloves,
Angie painted my mother's head
with bleach, a greasy paste,
then kneaded and sculpted the hair on top
into a Kewpie doll's one enormous curl.
She set the timer, as if boiling an egg.

If she left it on too long,
the hair would turn from auburn, red, blonde, silver
to my grandmother's snowy white.

I paged through the latest *Seventeen.*
April's Breck Girl gazed coolly back.
With her blonde pageboy
and pink cashmere sweater,
she looked like she belonged
in the white Cadillac double-parked out front.

She hated my babyish ponytail, too!
Today, I was having a little trim.
A semester short of his degree,
the boss's son practiced on me,
bending my neck backward
onto the cold pink lip of the basin.
His every touch gave me a shock.
Even while he snipped my hair,
I couldn't take my eyes off my mother's
bumpy rubber scalp stained with dyes
like bruises healing yellow-brown and plum.

If my mother had one life to live,
why not live it as a blonde?
Gone was her beautiful dark brown hair.
I had lost her
among the bottles of peroxide and shampoo,
rollers, bobby pins, rat-tailed combs,
and the dryers' swollen silver domes.

We walked the block back to the store,
one dark and one fair.
I kept checking that it was my mother—
passing the grocer, the butcher, the baker—
every window on the street a mirror.

When I was seventeen I had a vision of Christ.
One day I'd said something bad about God,
and by God I meant
the one I'd worshipped since Hebrew School,
God of the Burning Bush, the Red Sea Miracle,
the one-and-only God of the Old Testament.
That night I had a dream of me in my bedroom,
the very room in which I'm dreaming the dream,
and something wakes me, I look up and see—
projected on my white wall like the roll-up
screen on which my father shows home movies—
a picture moving, alive, streaked with pastels
like a page in my *Illustrated Children's Bible.*

Suddenly, I whirl around and see a stranger
sitting at my desk, handsome, young,
bare-chested, wearing a toga; there's sand
in his beard, on his feet between his toes,
on the blond leg hair wrapped
in the leather straps of his Jesus sandals,
the kind you could buy on 4th Street
in Greenwich Village. The funny thing is,
I recognize that he is Jesus, Jesus Christ,
and in my throat grows a gutteral, terrified cry;

and as I try to speak, he begins to rise,
seated in the same position,
as though an invisible string from the ceiling
pulls him three feet off the ground;

and as he begins to rise, I begin to sink,
in slow motion, I fall to my knees and bow
before him, breaking the commandment:
Thou shalt have no other gods before me.
Kneeling, I begin to cry, not a cry of sorrow
but a cry of joy, and he looks at me kindly
and says, in a gentle voice, in English,
It was so simple, you should have known all along.

I woke up shivering, alone; the luminous hands
on my Baby Ben alarm clock glowing 3:19.
I wanted to run to my parents' bedroom,
screaming, "I have just seen Jesus Christ!"
But first, I wanted him to send me a sign
that he was real, that it was *really* real—
what I had seen—I wanted a light to flash,
a picture to fall off the wall, a car horn
to honk three times from the street below.
Then I didn't want a sign. I didn't *want*
to think that it was real. If it were real,
I'd have to live, knowing that I'd seen Jesus.

What would the rabbi say?
Would my parents send me to a doctor,
lock me up in the loony bin?
Should I convert and live in a convent
with the other Jewish nuns from New Jersey?
How could I eat breakfast, lunch, and dinner,
and chew my food day after day after day?
Too frightened to fall asleep again,
by sunrise I had decided to try to forget it,
until one afternoon seven years later,

when sitting at a lecture in a dark auditorium,
a slide of Simone Martini's *Annunciation*
flashed huge on the projection screen—

the moment when the Archangel Gabriel
arrives from heaven to greet the Virgin,
interrupting her reading in the garden.
The golden words flying out of his mouth
head straight for the bull's-eye of her ear.
I recognized her shocked look, her awe,
the exact moment it dawns on her
that from now on she will never again be
the same person she woke up as that morning.

Then I knew it was Jesus Christ I'd seen,
not Gabriel, not David, or some wing'd
messenger from heaven God had sent.
I didn't have to wrestle Jacob's angel,
or offer a glass of water to a thirsty
stranger knocking on my door.
I knew what I had seen was real,
as real as the prayer book Mary was reading,
with the light falling on it and with shade
between the pages, when the Angel
took her by surprise: a real girl, my age,
a real angel, an angel real as Jesus—
as real as your fingers touching this page.

". . . Music minus the solo melody part—with the tapes or records providing the background music, you can play an instrument or sing along with the band, try your hand at Grand Opera, or even perform a concerto, surrounded by a full symphony orchestra."
—FROM THE *MUSIC MINUS ONE* CATALOGUE

Sunday afternoons, my father practiced
flute in the family room.
He warmed up, playing scales
while my mother worked the crossword puzzle
in her wing chair, like a throne.
Three o'clock and she was still
wearing her nightgown and slippers.
Our store downstairs was closed.
She was sick of looking at dresses all week.
Sunday was her day of rest.

I sprawled on the floor with my homework.
Each in our little orbit.
My father gave it all up when he married her.
Abdicated, like the Duke of Windsor.

Music was no life for a family man.
During the War, he had led the band
in the Marine Corps, in the South Pacific.
In the photo, each man poses with his instrument
except my father, holding a baton;
clarinets and saxophones leaning against their chests,
like rifles at port arms.

It was my job to start the record over.
The sheet music, stapled to the album cover,
was propped on the music stand.
The needle skated its single blade
in smaller and smaller circles on black ice.
The needle skipped. He was a little rusty.
When he lost his place, it left a hole in the music,
like silence in a conversation.

You had to imagine his life before the War.
At fifteen, on the Lower East Side, he played weddings
and bar mitzvahs;
at sixteen, he toured with the Big Bands.
You had to imagine him before
he changed his name from Joseph Sharfglass
to George Shore; you had to imagine him
handsome in his baby blue tuxedo
when he played with Clyde McCoy's orchestra
lighting up hotel ballrooms from New York to California
and all the road stops in between.
One enchanted evening in Connecticut,
he saw my mother.
A week later, he shipped off to the War.

You had to imagine his life before the War—
the one-night stands, the boys on the bus,
and in its wake the girls
with plucked eyebrows and strapless dresses
surrounding him like the mannequins
as he stood behind the counter
of his store, waiting for customers,
in New Jersey on the Palisades.

You had to imagine him occupying the uniform
now folded neatly in his footlocker
under the telescope pocked with rust—or bloodstains—
a souvenir from the War.
The record spun. He caught his breath.
The music raced on without him.

3

MEAT

The year I had the affair with X,
he lived downtown on Gansevoort Street,
in a sublet apartment over the warehouses.
They were considered chic places to live.
He was wavering over whether to divorce
his wife, and I'd fly down
every other week to help him decide.
Most nights, we'd drop in for cocktails
on the Upper East Side and hobnob
with his journalist friends, then taxi
down to Soho for an Opening and eat
late dinner in restaurants whose diners
wore leather and basic black.
We'd come home at four in the morning
just as it was starting to get light
and huge refrigerator trucks were backing up
to the loading docks and delivering
every kind of fresh and frozen meat.
Through locked window grates I could see
them carrying stiff carcasses, dripping crates
of iced chickens. We'd try to sleep
through the racket of engines and men
shouting and heavy doors being slammed.
By three in the afternoon the street would be
completely deserted, locked up tight;
at twilight they'd start their rounds again.
The street always smelled of meat.
The smell drifted past the gay bars
and parked motorcycles, it smelled

like meat all the way to the Hudson.
And though they hosed it down as best
they could, it still smelled as though
a massacre had occurred earlier that day,
day after day. We saw odd things
in the gutter—lengths of chain, torn
undershirts, a single shoe, and sometimes
even pieces of flesh—human or animal,
you couldn't tell—and blood puddling
around the cobbles and broken curbstones.
On weekends, we'd ask the taxi
to drop us off at the door
so that no one could follow and rob us.
We'd climb to our love nest
and drape a sheet over the bedroom window—
the barred window to the fire escape—
which faced across the airshaft the window
of a warehouse—empty, we assumed,
because we'd never seen lights on
behind the cracked and painted panes.
In the morning, we'd sleep late,
we'd take the sheet down and walk
around the apartment naked,
and eat breakfast in bed, and read,
and get back to our great reunions . . .
One Sunday, we felt something creepy—
a shadow, a flicker—move behind a corner
of broken glass. And we never knew
who they were, or how many,
or for how many months they had been
watching us, the spectacle we'd become.
Because that's what we were to them—

two animals in a cage fucking:
arms and backs and muscle
and flanks and sinew and gristle.

My sister is doing her exercises,
working out in my husband's study.
The rowing machine sighs deeply with every stroke,
its heavy breathing, like a couple making love.

She's visiting from Iowa
where the cold weather is much worse.

When she was ten, I'd hear her
strumming her guitar through the bedroom wall.
She'd borrow my albums—my Joan Baez, my Dylan—
and sing along,
shutting me out, drawing me in;
imitating my hair, my clothes,
my generation.

I used to feel sorry for her
for being eight years younger.

She opens the door a crack, and surfaces
in earphones, and wearing pink bikini panties
and a lover's torn T-shirt.
Strapped to her hands are the weights
that weighed her suitcase down.
Her thighs are tight, her triceps shine,
her body is her trophy.

The night she arrived, we sprawled across my bed,
her cosmetic bag spilled open
and she shadowed my eyelids violet,

demonstrating the latest tricks;
the way I used to make her up
on those nights she watched me dress for dates,

watched me slip into my miniskirt,
my sandals, my love beads.
Now she's no longer in love with me,
and eyes me pityingly,
triumphant, her expression the same as mine
when I watched my mother
examine her face in the magnifying mirror.

She's got to keep in shape.
She's a performer, it's her business
to look beautiful every night.
Sometimes, when she begins to sing,
men in the audience fall in love.

She's warming up in the shower;
the tile walls amplify her voice.
Safe, for once, under temperate rain.

Like a dress handed down
from sister to sister,
in time, one body will inherit
what the other has outgrown.

for Elizabeth Bishop

That afternoon on the Bay of Fundy,
as the car plunged in and out of the cobweb fog,
everything was in the process of erasing
or being erased.
At low tide, the tidal bore's puddle-raked mud flats
looked like a bolt of brown corduroy
running down the coast.
Later, when the sun came out, the puddles
turned into shattered mirrors, long shards;
blue sky and clouds lying in pieces on the ground,
as though the heavens had fallen down.

Stopping at a gas station for directions
and a Coke, my husband and I heard the local joke:
"You go from Upper Economy, to Middle, to Lower,
to Just Plain Broke."

The next day, on Cape Breton, pressed for time,
we wanted to drive the entire Cabot Trail
in a day. If we started at dawn
and drove clockwise around the coast,
we'd end up at dusk where we began.
The road linked town after coastal town,
each with its prim white clapboard church
starched stiff as a christening gown.
Azure woodsheds, chartreuse barns,
stilt houses shingled gray or shingled brown,

matchbox houses two stories high
painted the same pea green, ochre, or peacock blue
as the boats docked in the harbor below.
In Nova Scotia—nowhere else in the Maritimes—
fishermen paint their houses to match their boats!

It was like looking through the wrong end of a telescope,
everything scaled down, "smaller than life."
In Belle Côte, four wooden fishing boats
bobbed single file—gosling-style—
in the middle of the harbor
while real full-size fishing boats
bobbed, tethered to the dock.
Were they a practical joke—
or a winter evening's woodwork?
Those little boats looked too *serious* to be toys.
And that dollhouse stuck on a pole—
a whittled-down version of the gabled house
looming up behind it—
was really a mailbox!
No mail today. No one home.
Everyone seems to have vanished,
leaving their toys behind.

We counted more scarecrows than farmers
working in the fields.
No solitaries crucified on broompoles
meditating over a quarter acre of corn,
these posed in groups, in gay tableaux,
whole families of scarecrows
watching their gardens grow.
We drove past a family of scarecrow men
lovingly dressed in their Sunday best—

workshirts, overalls, and stovepipe hats.
Great-grandfather, Grandfather, Father, and Son
holding hands like a row of paper dolls,
passing on the deed to the farm—
to the last son, the current one,
stretching out his hand to thin air.

A few miles up the road
a scarecrow child was dressed for winter
in dungarees, sweater, mittens, and a scarf,
standing between his scarecrow mother and father
whose broomstick arm stuck out
in a permanent gesture of waving hello—or good-bye—
depending on the direction
you were driving to—or from.

That day, I was wearing an Indian cotton skirt
printed with huge vivid flowers.
A bee flew into the open window of the moving car
and tried to pollinate my skirt.

Given the modest scale of things,
whose idea was it to build
"the largest lobster trap in the world,"
a wooden scaffolding the size of a cathedral?
How many weathered traps had we seen
stacked by the side of the road?
A lobster trap?—it was a tourist trap!
Inside, a little gift shop
sold the usual array of junk:
lobster ashtrays, lobster key rings,
and foot-long lobster-claw combs.

Not nearly as grand, the crafts museum
masqueraded as a souvenir stand.
We arrived just before closing.
The curator had just taken out her teeth.
Tight-lipped but cheerful, she led us
through a room jammed from floor to ceiling
with antique spinning wheels.
It was like strolling through the inside of a clock.
She sat on a low stool, carding raw wool
into clouds that she proceeded to spin,
pumping her treadle like an organ pedal,
demonstrating, for at least the hundreth time that day,
one of the lost arts of the district,
kept just barely alive by her
and a few elderly lady volunteers.
Down the road lived her Micmac counterpart—
the last of her tribe who knew how
to weave baskets from sweet grass and porcupine quills.

Crayoned signs read, PLEASE DON'T TOUCH!
the swatches of Scottish tartans and coats of arms,
and the bagpipe, a droopy octopus.
Don't touch the yellowing scrimshaw,
the tiny ivory- and bone-handled tools
that tatted feverish edges on doilies and handkerchiefs
also on display. Don't touch the battered toys—
dolls, locomotives, decoys, and the love letter
whose frilly signature's a faded sepia lace.
In a separate glass case, a missionary's
English Micmac Dictionary, and a pair
of beaded moccasins with stiff enormous tongues.
Of course, you can't touch *them!*
Or the sand-encrusted gold doubloon

shipwrecked off the coast like the rising moon—
lost, all lost, and then recovered.

These children's faces printed on a milk carton—
a boy and a girl
smiling for their school photographs;
each head stuck atop a column
of vital statistics:
date of birth, height and weight, color
of eyes and hair.

On a carton of milk.
Half gallon, a quart.
Of what use is the body's
container, the mother weeping milk or tears.

No amount of crying will hold it back
once it has begun its journey
as you bend all night over the toilet,
over a fresh bowl of water.
Coins of blood spattering the tile floor
as though a murder had been committed.

Something wasn't right, they say,
you are lucky.
Too soon to glimpse the evidence
of gender, or to hear a heartbeat.

Put away the baby book, the list of names.
There are four thousand, at least, to choose from.
No need now to know their derivations,
their meanings.

Faces pass you in the supermarket
as you push the wire cart down the aisles.
The police artist flips through pages
of eyes and noses, assembling a face,
sliding the clear cellophane panels into place.

You take a quart of milk.
Face after face,
smiling obedient soldiers,
march in even rows
in the cold glass case.

Before she was born,
I was a woman who slept
through the night, who could live
with certain thoughts without collapsing . . .

if my husband died,
I could remarry; if I lost
my job, I could relocate,
start afresh . . .

I could live through "anything."
Even my daughter arriving
four weeks early,
a smile stitching my raw abdomen, hurting
as if I'd been cut in half.

When they brought her to me
for the first time, her rosiness
astonished me, she
who had been so long in the dark:

swathed in an absurd cap and a blanket
washed, rewashed, folded precisely as origami;
a diaper fan-folded to accommodate
her tiny body, a long-sleeved undershirt
with the cuffs folded over her perfect hands,
making them stumps.

In my private room
filled with expensive gift bouquets—
I hardly slept a wink—
the stalk-necked bird-of-paradise flowers,
blind under their spiky crowns of petals,
gawked at me, and the anthurium's
single heart-shaped bloodred leaf
dangled a skinny penis.

The next morning, they wheeled me to the nursery.
Behind the glass window,
the newborns were displayed, each
in its own clear plastic Isolette.
A few lay in separate cribs, under heat lamps,
and among them, mine
born thirty days early, scrawny, naked, her skin tinged
orange with jaundice.

Under the ultraviolet lamps, her eyes taped shut,
like a person in a censored photograph,
a strip of tape slapped over her genitalia,

a prisoner, anonymous, in pain—

my daughter, one day old, without a name,
splayed naked under the lamps,
soaking up the light of this world,
a sad sunbather stretched out on Waikiki.

4

At first, she seemed an apparition,
the white chiffon of her party dress,
the sheer moth-wings of her sleeves
caught in the web of our car beams.
The setting was perfect, a graveyard,
the weather, summer, slightly chilly,
a scene in a movie, a couple
driving home from a party,
a lonely country road, a woman
in distress, the decoy's murderous

accomplices hiding in the trees,
our good baby slumped in her padded
car seat in the back beside me.
You slowed the car to a crawl,
the tires crunching dirt and gravel.
Up close, she looked human enough;
the ghost a teenager, barely a woman.
You said quietly, without turning,
lock your door. In seconds,
the windshield fogged with breath.

Between gasps and sobs, she told
how she had been out driving alone,
and a car of boys—*of men*—she corrected,
had chased her up and down
the back roads, down the Calais Road,
the Jack Hill Road, the Pekin Branch,
forced her into a ditch, and run off.
Down the hill past the cemetery hedge
we saw the faint blush of taillights,
just as she'd said, and the tip

of tail fin sticking out of the ditch.
Should we take her to the hospital?
She was unhurt, she said.
Should we call the State Police?
Had she been raped?
Your foot poised on the gas pedal.
No, no, she said. You said, Get in.
She wedged herself into the backseat
with me, the baby cradled in the middle.
Reeking of liquor and cigarette smoke,

she shook as violently as our idling car.
What to do? I was new at being a mother.
Reaching across my sleeping daughter,
I shyly touched the girl's trembling arm
cold through the layer of chiffon,
and patted her, and petted her, like a cat,
while you asked her her name,
her phone number, the road she lived on.
Our road, how strange. She'd show us
the house. We passed her car, blue,

I'm the Thirteenth Fairy
who makes Sleeping Beauty
prick her finger on a spindle
and fall into Adolescence's deep sleep
from which she'll awaken,
years later as I did, as a mother.
Over and over, I watch my daughter
fall into a faint, and die.

"Rapunzel, Rapunzel," I call from below,
eye-level with the hem of the dust ruffle,
"Let down your hair!—"
and Emma solemnly flips her long beige braids
over the edge of the bed,
wearing a pair of my pantyhose on her head, like a wig.
The nylon feet softly brush the floor.
Now I am witch, now prince, now witch
climbing the pale ladder of Rapunzel's hair.
Pretending my fingers are scissors,
I lop off her braids, cutting off
the source of my daughter's power,
her means of escape, her route
to loving someone other than me.

Once, I played the heroine,
now look what I've become.
I am the one who orders my starving child
out of my house and into the gloomy woods,
my resourceful child, who fills her pockets
with handfuls of crumbs or stones
and wanders into a witch's candy cottage.

I am the one who sends my Vassilissa on an errand
from which it's doubtful she'll return alive
from a fate too horrible to say aloud,
a witch's hut built from her victims' bones.

I am the one who commands the hunter to kill,
and cut out my daughter's heart
and bring it back, posthaste,
the heart as proof.
I will salt it, and eat it.
I do this as a present for my daughter.
And like the good girl I started out as,
I mind my manners,
I lick the plate clean, lick it
clean and shiny as a mirror—
Time's talking mirror—who is my daughter.

THE SOUND OF SENSE

for Ann Moulton

Through the heat register I can hear
my daughter reading in the room below,
eating breakfast in her usual chair
at the kitchen table, two white pages
of her open book throwing the blinding
pan of sunlight back at her downcast face.
I hear her chirping up and down the scale
but I can't decipher a single word
as Emma learns to read. She's in first grade
and has to read a new book every day,
a weight she carries between school and back
home in her backpack, in a Ziploc
baggie, with her lunch—a nibbled sandwich
squashed into an aluminum foil ball
she's crumpled hard as a chunk of pyrite.
She unzips the baggie and out falls
"The Farm," eight pages long, more a pamphlet
than a book. Not much happens in the plot.
A farm, a barn, a boy, a cow that moos a lot.
The words are hard—but Emma sounds them out
one at a time, the *O*'s both long and short—
Cheerios bobbing in a lake of milk
in which her spoon trails like a drunken oar.
This morning her father, coaching her,
clears his throat, knocking his cup against *what?*
—I hear it clatter but can't make it out.
"Hurry up," he shouts, "or you'll miss the bus!"
I hear his imperative clear enough

but in the raised volume of her reply
the words are lost, garbled, caught in the throat
of the register's winding ducts and vents.
In an hour or so, when sunlight moves on,
a film will glaze the soured milk, like frost,
where the sodden *O*'s float, life preservers.
Now, over muffled clinks of silverware,
clattered plates, running water, morning din,
the sound of sense resumes its little dance.
I hear my daughter turn the title page,
then silence, then a spurt of words, false start,
then hesitance, a spondee of some sort,
then an iamb, then an anapest, then
a pause, another iamb—that's The End.
Then the scrape of wood on tile as Emma
pushes her chair away and clomps upstairs
to change from her pajamas into clothes.

THE MOON ROSE ORANGE

for Barry and Lorrie Goldensohn

There are times I've seen it rise yellow
over the mountain, twice its normal size.
But tonight the moon rose orange as the tip
of a lit cigarette, and slowly as it climbs,
it silences the fields below the house,
illuminates the barn, the granite steps
that Wilfred Peck a hundred years ago
dragged from the lower fields to the porch
of now rotted boards and shaky railings.
I'll bet Will used to come out here to think
and smoke after his family went to sleep.
He'd light his pipe—watching the flame
burrow in the tamped tobacco—blow out
the match, and pitch it over the rail.
I doubt he ever dreamed that a city girl
could love his father's land as much as he.
Will's oldest daughter, Charlotte Jackman,
sold it to the Bassages up the road
who sold it to Toby Knox who sold it
to Greg Mosher who sat at his kitchen
table over cups of coffee and shook hands
with my husband, and it was ours.
One day, our daughter will own it, too.

They're both sleeping; the refrigerator hums.
The barn's still standing but the cows are gone.
The upper pasture where they used to graze

clear to the trout pond ledge has turned to woods.
Gone, too, the corncrib, and the silo,
the snaking line of children, some on sleds,
parading from the village—called Moscow then—
down snowy Route 14 and up Peck Hill
to boil sap where the sugarhouse once stood.
Our porch still affords the perfect view.
In the distance, the church's white steeple
punctuates the village's one sentence
of gas pumps, general store, PO—same
buildings Will drove his team of horses past
on his way to Hardwick to purchase grain.

Somebody gave Will's portrait to the town.
Founders Day, they tacked it to the wall
of the Meeting House on Gospel Hollow Road.
Shyly, I glanced at him—mustached, married,
handsome, in his twenties? early thirties?
(old enough to be my great-grandfather—
but with fair hair and aquiline nose), Will
leans against the parlor wall the Knoxes
tore down to enlarge their living room.
I wanted to take his photograph
and hang it in our house, where it belongs.

Last winter, when we were insulating walls,
my husband came running to show me
what the carpenter found in the attic,
stuffed in with newspapers between the laths,
a second-grade primer singed with mildew,
Will Peck in pencil on the flyleaf—
penmanship the same as my eight-year-old's.
When Scott Bassage's parents owned the house,

they found two old farm diaries of Will's,
dated eighteen ninety-four and ninety-five.
Scott loaned them to us the week we moved in.
Compact as billfolds, their tan canvas covers
look barely touched; on the frontispiece
in rickety penciled loops, Will the man's
signature hasn't changed from Will the boy's.

Paging through his diary at night in bed,
I thumb past Tide Charts, Phases of the Moon,
the Zodiac, Calendar, Weights and Measures,
Antidotes for Poisons, Rates of Postage
(letters from here to Boston cost two cents),
The Presidents of the United States
(from George Washington to Grover Cleveland).
As if Will distrusted the permanence of ink,
his pencil plows between the narrow lines—
cash accounts, animals bought and sold,
wages paid to Clarence, the hired man.
With two fingers I could eclipse Will's day—
MONDAY, APRIL 9, 1894
Churned butter in the forenoon, it rained,
lazed about the rest of the afternoon.
FRIDAY, MAY 4 *Planted potatoes.*
Mother got pretty tired. Doctor came.
WEDNESDAY, AUGUST 10 *Father Bliss and I*
went to Plainfield after a load of coal
in the forenoon and a load of sawdust
in the afternoon; I fixed the fence.
I see his pencil press the period,
a breath away—and beg him not to haunt
my house. And yet, I wish I could stand
on the porch, and light a cigarette

as I used to, before smoking was dangerous.
I'd wrap a blanket around my shoulders
and invite Will to pass the time with me,
and watch the moon, happy for his company.

We filed through the exhibits,
Charlotte and I taking turns
reading captions to Andy.
Herded into a freight elevator,
we rode to the top floor,
to the beginning of the War

where we were on our own,
descending floor by floor,
year by year, into history
growing darker, ceilings
lowering, aisles narrowing
to tunnels like the progress

of Andy's vision over the years.
In Warsaw, his family owned
Maximillian's Fur Salon,
like a little Bergdorf Goodman's,
doorman and French elevator,
furs draped on the Persian carpet,

over the blue velvet Empire chairs.
Andy was one of the lucky ones,
a Jewish boy escaping Poland
the day before the border closed;
playing card games with his cousin
in the backseat of the family Packard

as they inched through peasant villages,
trading mink coats for gasoline.
If his German shepherd guide dog,
Topper, isn't there, it's hard to tell
that Andy is blind, Andy's blue eyes
look normal, and he stares

directly at you when you speak.
His bearded face, grave, listening,
as Charlotte and I stood to the side
describing photographs or reading
softly, quickly, in monotones,
so as not to attract attention,

casually, as if reading selections
from a menu. Guards warned us
that there were so many things to see—
thousands of bits of information,
photographs, newsreels, movies—
it would take us days to read it all.

That morning, I had dressed
in a black sweater and black pants,
black coat and black boots,
and Charlotte and Andy had, too,
mourners attending a mass funeral.
I knew that, eventually,

something had to break me down—
the cattle car, the crematorium door,
the confiscated valises of Jews
piled high and dramatically lit
as in a department store display,
or the room filled with nothing

but shoes—mountains of shoes—
each shoe still shaped to the human
foot it had once belonged to,
a man's shoe, a woman's shoe,
a left or a right shoe, its mate
lost in a pile somewhere;

dusty, scuffed boots and pumps,
heels worn down to the shank,
shoes that appeared to have walked
miles and miles to arrive here.
The odd thing was—
the room smelled like feet.

I managed not to cry.
Until a small snapshot of a girl
shot dead, lying beside her family
on a cobbled street—her hair
as long as my eight-year-old's,
her coat, my daughter's size—

stopped my words, and by then
Charlotte had started crying
and Andy was crying, too.
I didn't ask what had triggered
each private grief.
When I couldn't read, Charlotte

would continue mid-sentence,
when she choked up and had to stop,
I stepped in. We started developing
a rhythm, Andy's hand placed
on Charlotte's or my arm to guide him
through room after room of empty air.

Around us, weeping strangers
detoured around our little group
moving far too slow for them;
and as they passed they stared
openly at Andy
knowing he couldn't stare back,

but they *smiled* at Topper straining
against his leash and metal harness,
they *chuckled* when Topper flopped
down sighing and nodding off
in the dark at Andy's feet
each time we stopped to read.

A woman asked permission to pet him.
After those nightmare photographs
of snarling, muzzled, killer dogs,
what a relief to see
an ordinary one,
and something that wasn't human.

Three o'clock. We were starved,
but nobody felt like eating.
Charlotte and I went to the ladies room
leaving Topper and Andy in the lobby
by the cloakroom, near a black family
putting on their coats.

The husband wanted to pet Topper,
and struck up a conversation
with Andy. "I see you're blind,"
he said politely. "Do you understand this
any better than I do?" And Andy
shook his head and told him no.

After dinner, while the coffee perked
and my mother cleared the dishes,
my father would take from the shelf
the Scrabble box and the dictionary,
its black leatherette jacket as battered
as some *other* family's heirloom Bible,
its red ribbon bookmark frayed to arterial threads.

I'd sprawl on the floor a few feet away
and start to do my homework.
My father unfolded the game board
onto the lazy Susan's wooden turntable,
and shuffled the wooden Scrabble tiles
face down in the box.

They'd be seated in their usual places
at the dining table—husband opposite wife.
Aunt Flossie would select seven tiles from the box,
her hand skimming them like a clairvoyant's.
Then Uncle Al, to her left, would draw.
He was used to arguing cases in court,
and always winning, like Perry Mason.

Waiting his turn,
he'd bully my father about his tie,
insult my mother's coffee,
comment about my beatnik-long hair.
Then, he'd start an argument with my aunt
—in front of everyone—
adjusting his black pirate-patch

over his missing right eye,
like the Hathaway Shirt man modeling in *Life*.

I'd get up and circle the table.
Standing behind my mother's back,
I studied the letters on her rack,
her ever-changing cache of luck—
syllables, stutters, false starts,
the game's only Z or X, or Q—useless without a U
unless you were spelling IRAQ, and then
no foreign words or proper nouns allowed.
She added an S to the board, going across,
and a ROSE grew into a bouquet.
Under the S, she put T-A-R,
and it spawned a STAR, going down.
My mother held in reserve her secret weapon—
a blank tile—that could substitute
for any letter in the alphabet.
They all bickered while she announced her score
and rotated the lazy Susan a quarter turn.

A ten-minute limit—that was their rule—
ten minutes to come up with a word.
Ten minutes. Ten minutes. Ten minutes.
Another half-hour passed.

Ashtrays filled up, were emptied,
ashes drifting over the vinyl tablecloth
as, week after month after year,
the lazy Susan turned under the chandelier.
They'd play until ten or eleven, or until Al blew up
and my aunt tried to smooth things over,
my mother muttering "some things will never change."

But once, before I went off to college,
I witnessed them actually finish a game.

Uncle Al stared at his letters.
Aunt Flossie lit up a cigarette,
and asked, "What's with Milton Marx?"
My mother said, "I saw him in the pharmacy.
Two days out of the hospital, he looks terrible."
My father said, "He stopped by the store.
To me, he looked okay."
My uncle said, "Milton called me on the phone.
He could barely even talk, he was so hoarse."
My aunt glanced at her rack of letters.
"Thank you very much!" Aunt Flossie said,
and quickly put HOARSE down on the board.

With the flat of his hand,
my father swept the letters back into the box,
and folded the board.
Uncle Al tallied up the final scores,
the fingernails on his elegant hands
buffed and polished from his weekly manicure.
He was *ambidextrous*—
a talent he was proud of,
a word that would make a killing.

I carried it in my wallet,
the way teenage boys used to carry
a single condom—just in case.

On my visits home, after dessert,
my father would nod to my mother,
my younger sister, my aunts, my uncle,
and, catching my eye, he'd give me the signal—a wink.
He'd stand up, excusing us
from all the coffee drinkers at the table.
The two of us would go downstairs,
unlock the store, deactivate the alarm,
and lock the door behind us,
making sure we were alone.

I'd follow him past the dress racks
into the last fitting room in the back.
He'd draw the curtain,
unlatch the door disguised by a mirror,
and then, he'd point to the family safe
hidden under a green drape,
always prefacing his apology
with, "It's only just in case,
in case something should happen,
I'm no spring chicken, let's face it."
And then he'd shrug.

I'd kneel before the squat steel box.
While he shone the flashlight on my hands,
nervous, I practiced the routine

I'd rehearsed for the last twenty years,
ever since he'd had his heart attack.
Every time the heavy door swung open,
I'd close my eyes, not wanting to look inside.

When my aunt called,
I drove north all day, checking my wallet,
checking the numbers he'd jotted down
still legible on the torn pink slip.

Behind the faded GOING OUT OF BUSINESS sign
he had placed in the window
a month before my mother had died,
the empty store was a tomb,
the upstairs apartment was a tomb,
the safe had been moved to his closet.
Underneath the chorus line of laundered shirts,
lay the green drape shrouding the safe.

I got down on my knees.
I started with the dial turned to 0.
I turned the dial to the left two whole turns
and stopped at 79.
I turned the dial to the right one whole turn
and stopped at 35.
I turned the dial to the left
and stopped at 10.
I heard a click, turned the handle,
and pulled open the heavy door.

In the sliding metal drawers and shelves,
sets of keys and stacked envelopes
stuffed with green, with gold

cuff links, his gold wedding ring
and gold Jewish Star I'd seen him wear
every day of my life,
his dog tags, expired membership cards—
musician's union, driver's license,
smeary photocopies of birth certificates,
and the key to the safety-deposit box,
(the duplicate key I'd locked in mine
after my sister and I
divided up our mother's jewelry)—

everything on the up and up,
no mistresses, no skeletons, a life
apparently as orderly
as the inside of this safe.

—All those years of spinning the numbers,
rehearsing the combination—
father, mother, daughter, daughter—
until I got it right.

A year before she died, my mother began cutting herself
out of the picture. Scissors in hand,
she littered the family room floor with snapshots.
In the group picture of Table Four taken at the wedding
someone in the last row is missing.
I can trace the jagged outline of her absent hip and arm.

My daughter and I are doing a project.
I tear the cellophane off the cardboard box
and spread before me on the kitchen table
a model kit of the human female body.
She is called The Visible Woman.
She is the partner of The Visible Man.
They resemble each other in every way
except for the reproductive organs
and the removable breastplate and optional parts
to simulate a baby in the womb.

Which is where I come in. She is living
on High Street, in Newark, New Jersey.
The War is over. She has married my father.
At thirty-one, she is considered old
to be having her first baby.
In the black-and-white photos, she lathers my body
suspended in the hammock of a bassinet.
I see her wedding ring.
Her head is legitimately missing,
cropped, beyond the frame.

The right eye and the left eye have to be cemented
into the proper sockets in the skull.
We swathe the table with newspapers, assemble our tools:
glue, paints, knife, tweezers, toothpicks,
brush, rubber bands, and clothespins.

At the factory, the body parts
have been sorted into separate plastic bags.
They look like pieces of broken porcelain.
Light as jackstraws,
the 206 individual bones of the skeleton
have names—mandible, ulna, tibia, patella—
like flowers, and not like the names of bones.
With a hinge pin, I attach the right foot to the fibula.
My daughter runs her fingers over the rib cage
as if plucking a melody on a comb.

"The foot bone's connected to the leg bone.
The leg bone's connected to the thigh bone."
Dancing the hootchie-kootchie,
my mother liked to sing me this silly song.
She liked when I played the piano,
and like a torch singer, she could croon,
"There's a small hotel by a wishing well,"
which embarrassed me,
reminding me of her honeymoon.

The vital organs are pink and the skeleton is ivory.
It's my job to tuck the liver, kidney, and heart
into the transparent half shells of the skin.
With nothing to fill it, it is nearly invisible.

She stopped singing. The year before she died,
we didn't talk much on the phone,
her voice disembodied, searching
for a neutral subject.
When I'd call and ask to speak with her,
my father said that she was "indisposed."
She shut me out, hung up on my life, the line went dead.
So I missed it all, the tubes, the nosebleeds.

On the tip of my paintbrush
hangs one drop of glossy red enamel.
I have to paint red lines and blue lines,
the routes to and from the heart.

She lost her hair.
She lost her appetite, and started disappearing.
My mother, who had dieted her whole life long,
slimmed down to a svelte size ten.
She could finally eat anything on earth,
but she didn't want to.
She didn't want me to see
her bald head as smooth and white
as the Styrofoam wig stand
I found in a box in her closet
the day after she died.

She lost her mother
in the 1918 flu epidemic, when she was three.
So what could she know of mothering?
She gave me this advice, when I was growing up,
"Never trust women,
they'll knife you in the back."

And so I didn't get to see her
in the hospital, I didn't get to see
the metal walker she leaned on,
when she was too dizzy to stand.
I didn't get to see her
swaying in front of the washing machine,
not knowing which dial to turn.

My father had to close the clasp of her necklace.
Her fingers "didn't work."
Her signature, on the last birthday card she sent me,
straggling.

My aunt Flossie said, "She's lost some weight,
but her color's good."

> *The instruction manual recommends the following colors:*
> *white, yellow, red, blue, and brown.*
> *The chart says to paint the lung mottled a light blue,*
> *the ovaries yellow,*
> *the aorta red,*
> *the pancreas grayish white,*
> *the spleen dark reddish brown,*
> *the gall bladder light green,*
> *the umbilical cord light blue.*

In home movies, in color photographs,
in black and white, into the grays of life, she faded.
Days after the funeral,
I thought I smelled her in her bedroom,
haunted by her perfume, Je Reviens.

I gave her brassieres and panties to the Salvation Army.
I kept the clothes that fit me.
Three years later, wearing her sweater,
fishing in the right-hand pocket,
I found a clump of her wadded blue Kleenex.

I agreed to "respect her wishes"
and not visit her.
She said that she "didn't have the strength" to see me.
I asked my aunts to beg for me.

I argued with her about it on the phone.
I pleaded with her to let me come home.
She discouraged me
from attending Aunt Lil's funeral,
but I came, anyway, and watched her
stare vacantly at the hole in the ground.
She stared as they lowered the coffin.
Later, sitting in our family room, in her usual chair,
she stared straight ahead for hours,
as if having her portrait painted.
She stared, except for when my daughter
made her smile.

I watched her eat lunch at the kitchen table.
I watched her shave two slices off a block of cheese,
put them into her mouth,
and try to swallow.
I gulped for her, and asked,
"Don't you want to talk with someone professional
about your illness?"
"I never think about it," was her reply.

The last time I saw her,
she was standing outside the front door,
in front of the windows of our store
that my father had closed a month before.
Cars and buses going by,
the traffic light flashing green
then yellow then red.

She was wearing her blue nightgown and slippers,
her wig, like a bowler hat, slightly askew;
woozy, tipsy as a drunk, she waved good-bye.

> *The Visible Woman is ready to be assembled.*
> *The paint is no longer tacky.*
> *Closing her jawbone, I lower her skeleton*
> *into the body shell, in the correct order*
> *so the parts will fit.*
> *I snap her stomach and her intestines into this cavity*
> *where they fit together, perfectly.*
> *She comes with her own pedestal.*

On the phone the last words she said to me,
"Have a nice life."

Jane Shore grew up in North Bergen, New Jersey. Her first book of poems, *Eye Level*, won the 1977 Juniper Prize; and her second book, *The Minute Hand*, won the 1986 Lamont Poetry Prize, awarded by The Academy of American Poets. She received a fellowship from The John Simon Guggenheim Foundation, and was a Fellow in Poetry at The Mary Ingraham Bunting Institute (formerly The Radcliffe Institute), an Alfred Hodder Fellow at Princeton University, a Goodyear Fellow at The Foxcroft School in Middleburg, Virginia, and a Jenny McKean Moore Writer-in-Washington at The George Washington University in Washington, D.C. She has twice received grants from The National Endowment for the Arts.

Jane Shore was a Briggs-Copeland Lecturer on English at Harvard University, and was a Visiting Distinguished Poet at The University of Hawaii. Her poems have been published in numerous magazines, including *Poetry* (for which she received The Bess Hokin Award), *The New Republic, Ploughshares,* and *The Yale Review.* She currently teaches at The George Washington University and lives in Washington, D.C., and in Vermont with her husband, the novelist Howard Norman, and their daughter, Emma.